C000148952

1,000,000 Books

are available to read at

www.ForgottenBooks.com

Read online
Download PDF
Purchase in print

ISBN 978-0-428-13729-8
PIBN 11248299

This book is a reproduction of an important historical work. Forgotten Books uses
state-of-the-art technology to digitally reconstruct the work, preserving the original format
whilst repairing imperfections present in the aged copy. In rare cases, an imperfection in
the original, such as a blemish or missing page, may be replicated in our edition. We do,
however, repair the vast majority of imperfections successfully; any imperfections that
remain are intentionally left to preserve the state of such historical works.

Forgotten Books is a registered trademark of FB &c Ltd.
Copyright © 2018 FB &c Ltd.
FB &c Ltd, Dalton House, 60 Windsor Avenue, London, SW19 2RR.
Company number 08720141. Registered in England and Wales.

For support please visit www.forgottenbooks.com

1 MONTH OF
FREE
READING

at
www.ForgottenBooks.com

By purchasing this book you are eligible for one month membership to ForgottenBooks.com, giving you unlimited access to our entire collection of over 1,000,000 titles via our web site and mobile apps.

To claim your free month visit:
www.forgottenbooks.com/free1248299

* Offer is valid for 45 days from date of purchase. Terms and conditions apply.

English
Français
Deutsche
Italiano
Español
Português

www.forgottenbooks.com

Mythology Photography **Fiction**
Fishing Christianity **Art** Cooking
Essays Buddhism Freemasonry
Medicine **Biology** Music **Ancient
Egypt** Evolution Carpentry Physics
Dance Geology **Mathematics** Fitness
Shakespeare **Folklore** Yoga Marketing
Confidence Immortality Biographies
Poetry **Psychology** Witchcraft
Electronics Chemistry History **Law**
Accounting **Philosophy** Anthropology
Alchemy Drama Quantum Mechanics
Atheism Sexual Health **Ancient History**
Entrepreneurship Languages Sport
Paleontology Needlework Islam
Metaphysics Investment Archaeology
Parenting Statistics Criminology
Motivational

Historic, archived document

Do not assume content reflects current
scientific knowledge, policies, or practices.

aper No. 16

December 1954

MORTALITY FOLLOWING PARTIAL CUTTING
IN VIRGIN LODGEPOLE PINE

By Robert R. Alexander

LIBRARY
CURRENT SERIAL RECORD

★ FEB 18 1955 ★

U. S. DEPARTMENT OF AGRICULTURE

U. S. DEPARTMENT OF AGRICULTURE

FOREST SERVICE

ROCKY MOUNTAIN FOREST AND RANGE EXPERIMENT STATION,

FORT COLLINS, COLORADO

Raymond Price, Director

COVER PICTURE -- Trees blown down by the first winds of gale intensity which followed partial cutting in lodgepole pine. This plot had a 4,000 board-foot per acre reserve volume in 1940. Picture taken in July 1943 shows destruction wrought by gales of January and May of that year.

MORTALITY FOLLOWING PARTIAL CUTTING IN VIRGIN LODGEPOLE PINE
by
R. R. Alexander, Forester
Rocky Mountain Forest and Range Experiment Station[1]

- - - - - - -

C O N T E N T S

	Page
Description of the area	1
Design of the experiment	2
Cutting intensities	2
How the data were collected	4
Results	4
Discussion	8
Summary	8

In 1939 a study of several intensities of partial cutting in the lodgepole pine type was started on the Fraser Experimental Forest in Colorado. Observation of mortality following logging has been one of the objectives of this study. Mortality and the agencies that cause it are often among the most important considerations in selecting the silvicultural system most suitable for any forest type. Growth of the reserve stand and adequate regeneration must also be considered in determining the suitability of a particular silvicultural system.

Heavy mortality following harvest cutting in virgin lodgepole pine (Pinus contorta) has been observed frequently. The species characteristically forms nearly pure, even-aged, or even-sized stands on slopes and ridges where soils are shallow. Logging of such stands often results in heavy windthrow if part of the original stand is left as a reserve. When such mortality is excessive it may offset satisfactory growth of the reserve stand and result in little or no net increment in volume per acre.

DESCRIPTION OF THE AREA

The study area lies in a small watershed between elevations of 9,150 to 9,700 feet. Topography is variable, changing from gentle slopes to slopes as steep as 45 degrees. Slope aspect varies from north to southwest and southeast. Soils are derived from schist, gneiss, and glacial till, and are coarse textured. There is no solid rock close to the surface that would prevent root penetration.

Prevailing westerly winds are normally gentle. At frequent intervals, however, heavy windstorms reach gale intensity. A study to determine the direction of these destructive winds, on another watershed adjacent to the plots showed that these storms come from the west.[2]

[1] Forest Service, U. S. Department of Agriculture, with headquarters at Colorado A & M College, Fort Collins, Colorado.
[2] Alexander, R. R., and Buell, J. H. Determining the Direction of Destructive Winds in a Rocky Mountain Timber Stand. Accepted for publication in the Journal of Forestry.

They are not modified by either the high range of mountains surrounding the area or by local topography within the watershed.

The original overstory was typical old-growth lodgepole pine, with a mixture of Engelmann spruce (Picea engelmannii) and subalpine fir (Abie lasiocarpa) on the more moist sites. The stand contained a large proport of low-vigor trees, but had not reached the stage of overmaturity where t overstory breaks up and reproduction invades the openings. The original understory was composed of pine, spruce, and fir seedlings, saplings, and poles along with a scattering of quaking aspen (Populus tremuloides). T. understory pine was generally too severely suppressed or too old to respo: to release.

The total stand contained between 300 and 400 trees per acre. Tre ranged from the smallest recorded diameter of 3.6 inches to an average ma mum diameter of 22 inches. Dominant trees averaged 80 to 85 feet in heigl Before cutting, merchantable volumes in trees larger than 9.5 inches in diameter varied from 7,600 to 17,000 board-feet per acre on individual plots, with an average of 12,000 for all plots. Total basal area varied considerably less; maximum basal area was 166.6 square feet per acre, the minimum 146.3; and the average, 158.4.

DESIGN OF THE EXPERIMENT

The study consists of four different cutting treatments with a cor sponding check area. Each treatment is replicated 4 times on plots 5 acr in size. Each 5-acre plot is surrounded by an isolation strip 1 chain wi: that received the same treatment as the plot. Four treated and one isolation plot comprise a randomized block. The 20 plots are scattered over the st area, but, except for minor variations, lie on moderate north to northwes slopes. (See map.)

CUTTING INTENSITIES

Commercial clearcutting

This treatment removed all trees larger than 9.5 inches in diamete regardless of species and vigor. This system of cutting was included wit the following partial cuttings so that it could be compared with them und similar conditions.

2,000 board-foot reserve volume

A growing stock of 2,000 board-feet per acre of the thriftiest tre larger than 9.5 inches in diameter was left. In selecting trees for the reserve stand, spacing, form, and external defect such as crook, porcupin damage, fire scars, and forking, were considered along with vigor. This method simulates a scattered seed-tree cutting, but differs in that no special attention was given to a tree's capacity to produce seed.

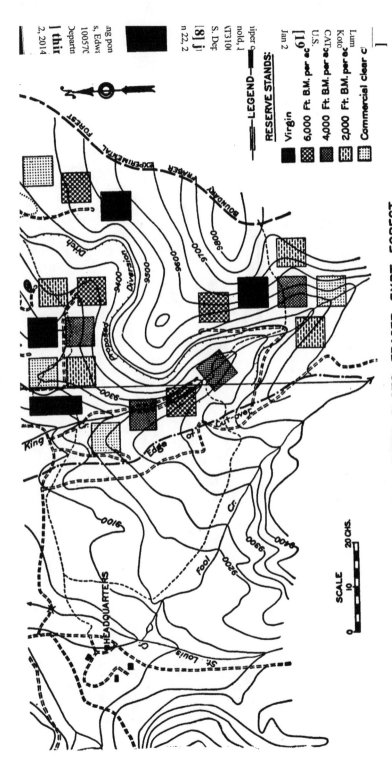

LODGEPOLE PINE HARVEST CUTTING PLOTS, FRASER EXPT. FOREST

MED
11:41c

CTRL
1/23/14

4,000 board-foot reserve volume

The only difference between this and the preceding system of cutting is in the reserve stand. Two thousand additional board-feet per acre were selected from the better trees to be left in the growing stock. This method resembles a very heavy selection or a modified shelterwood cutting. It seeks not only to insure adequate restocking of the area, but to control the number of seedlings and the development of poles in the understory as well.

6,000 board-foot reserve volume

This method of cutting removed approximately one-half of the original volume of 12,000 board-feet per acre in trees larger than 9.5 inches in diameter. The best trees were left as a reserve, but these necessarily included many low-vigor trees. This method of cutting simulates the initial step of a shelterwood cutting in which subsequent cutting is governed by the amount of reproduction that becomes established and the growth of the reserve stand.

True selection cutting, which would leave volumes of 8,000 to 10,000 board-feet per acre, was not included because the bulk of the volume was in trees over 200 years old. The general vigor of the stand was therefore too low to make such cutting feasible.

Uncut check

This treatment was included to provide a basis by which stand changes resulting from the removal of timber in the other treatments might be detected and analyzed.

In addition to the major treatments, improvement cutting was applied to trees 3.5 to 9.5 inches in diameter on one-half of each plot. This consisted of the removal of all defective trees and the thinning of dense groups of young poles. (This minor treatment was made to determine the effect of such cutting on the rate of growth and structure of the stand within major treatments. Stand improvement affected the density of the residual stand, but the effect on mortality was not isolated.)

The number of trees and basal area per acre in the reserve stand left after each major treatment and accompanying stand improvement are shown in the following tabulation.

Treatment	Reserve stand	
	Trees per acre	Basal area in sq. ft.
Commercial clearcutting	138	36.3
2,000 board-foot reserve	3/ 203	3/ 64.1
4,000 board-foot reserve	167	64.8
6,000 board-foot reserve	226	91.4
Uncut check	362	155.6

3/ The anomaly of more trees and nearly equal basal area on the plots cut to a 2,000 board-foot reserve when compared to the plots cut to a 4,000 board-foot reserve is explained by a larger number of trees below the merchantable limit on the 2,000 board-foot reserve plots.

HOW THE DATA WERE COLLECTED

After the plots were logged in the fall and winter of 1939-40, a survey of mortality was made in each of 4 years during a 12-year period (1940-51); namely in 1942, 1943, 1947, and 1951. For purposes of analysis the 1942 and 1943 surveys were combined to organize the 12-year periods into three 4-year periods, as follows: Period number 1, 1940-43, inclusive; period number 2, 1944-47, inclusive; and period number 3, 1948-51, inclusive.

Mortality was recorded by the following causes: windthrow (trees uprooted by the wind) and windbreak (trees broken at some point along the stem); insects (bark beetles); and miscellaneous causes. The miscellaneous mortality class included trees killed by logging damage, suppression, porcupines, disease, and unknown causes.

In addition to mortality, surveys of reproduction were made in 1939, 1941, and 1947, and an inventory of growth was made in 1947.

RESULTS

It was apparent from the growth inventory made 7 years after logging that lodgepole pine was not adapted to heavy partial cutting. Table 1 shows average net annual increment was either negligible or minus for all treatments. A reserve stand of 6,000 board-feet per acre, which normally would be considered windfirm, showed a net growth of only 1 board-foot per acre per year. Heavier partial cuttings which left reserve volumes of 4,000 and 2,000 board-feet per acre actually suffered a reduction in board-foot volumes, for growth failed to offset mortality. On the commercial clearcut plots, average net annual increment per acre though small was positive because of ingrowth and the lack of merchantable-size trees to be lost by death. Net growth on the check plots averaged 13.5 board-feet per acre per year.

Table 1.-- Average annual increment per acre under
different intensities of cutting (7 years)

Cutting treatment	Increment -- board-feet
Commercial clearcut	+11.4
2,000 board-foot reserve	-57.3
4,000 board-foot reserve	-63.7
6,000 board-foot reserve	+ 1.0
Uncut check	+13.5

The low or negative increment on all plots was due to high average annual mortality coupled with the inherent slow growth of lodgepole pine of all diameter classes. Previous studies of growth in selectively cut lodgepole pine stands have indicated that the average annual mortality per acre was 31 board-feet.[4] In table 2, where average annual mortality

[4] Hornibrook, E. M. A Preliminary Yield Table for Selectively Cut Lodgepole Pine Stands. Jour. Forestry 38: 641-643. 1940.

s given by treatments, mortality exceeded previous estimates by
approximately 3 times. The greatest loss occurred on the plots cut to
a reserve volume of 4,000 board-feet per acre, the lowest on the check
plots. The 2,000 and 6,000 board-foot reserve plots suffered approximately the same amount of loss.

Table 2.-- Average annual mortality per acre

Cutting treatment	Mortality -- board-feet
2,000 board-foot reserve	88.3
4,000 board-foot reserve	134.1
6,000 board-foot reserve	89.6
Uncut check	65.5

Reproduction inventories showed that lodgepole pine will regenerate
well under a variety of cutting treatments. Logging destroyed about one-
half of the advanced reproduction, leaving the plots one-third stocked.
Seven years later the number of seedlings and saplings had increased three-
fold, and more than 60 percent of all cutover plots were stocked.

Lodgepole pine has demonstrated that it can be reproduced adequately,
but mortality is excessive under partial cutting. Mortality in the lodgepole
pine type has received little attention in the past. Its extent and the
agencies that cause it are known only in a casual way.

In analyzing mortality on the Fraser plots, three main factors were
considered: (1) cause of death; (2) time since cutting; and (3) intensity
of cutting. Number of trees and basal area were used to express mortality
because trees in the 3.6- to 9.5-inch diameter classes would not be given
sufficient consideration if board-foot volumes were used as the basis of
analysis.

Causes of mortality during 12 years of observation are shown in table 3.
More than 16 percent of the total number of trees and basal area left in the
residual growing stock on all plots was lost. Windthrown and windbroken
trees accounted for more than three-fourths of the total loss. Windfall
varied considerably within a block and between blocks, but was always the
greatest cause of death.

Table 3.-- Causes of mortality (1940-51)

Cause	Total losses on 100 acres of plots during 12 years		Percentage of post-treatment growing stock lost		Percentage of losses from all causes		Average loss per acre per year	
	Trees	Basal area	No. of trees	Basal area	No. of trees	Basal area	Trees	Basal area
	No.	Sq.ft.	Pct.	Pct.	Pct.	Pct.	No.	Sq.ft.
Wind	2,518	1,073.4	11.5	13.0	70.0	77.5	2.1	0.9
Insects	753	245.8	3.5	3.0	21.0	18.0	0.6	0.2
Misc.	315	64.3	1.5	1.0	9.0	4.5	0.3	0.1
All	3,586	1,383.5	16.5	17.0	100.0	100.0	3.0	1.2

Wind losses were heaviest on plots that straddle ridge tops or lie
on exposed slopes. Windthrown trees ranged from spindly-stemmed and small-
crowned poles to large dominant trees with full crowns. Losses were about
equally divided among diameter and crown classes regardless of treatment
or exposure.

Insect losses were second to wind in importance, but were much
less. Losses from miscellaneous causes were minor and confined for the
most part to suppression of submerchantable trees.

No precise records are available on wind velocity in the lodgepole
pine type. Observation has indicated that a storm of gale intensity can
be expected as often as every 5 years. The frequency may vary between
localities, but there are relatively few instances where cutover stands of
lodgepole pine have escaped destructive winds shortly after logging.

The probability of frequent storms of such intensity and the importance
of wind as a cause of mortality in cutover stands raises an important question
What is the relationship between the amount of windfall and the time interval
since cutting? Do wind losses reach a peak at the time of first heavy windstorms after cutting and then decrease, or do they continue to increase in
relation to the time since cutting? If windfall losses continued undiminished
complete destruction of residual growing stock would soon result.

Wind losses per acre by treatments for 4-year periods are shown in
table 4. It is apparent from the table that heavy windfall was confined
to the first 4-year period under all intensities of cutting. Only 4 years
after logging all plots had suffered more than three-fourths of the total
number of tree and basal-area losses that occurred during the first 12 years
after cutting.

Table 4.-- Wind losses per acre by 4-year periods

Treatment	1940-43 4 years		1944-47 4 years		1948-51 4 years		1940-51 12 years		1940-51 loss as percent of post-treatment growing stock	
	Trees	Basal area	Trees	Basal area	Trees	Basal area	Trees	Basal area	No. of trees	Basal area
	No.	Sq.ft.	No.	Sq.ft.	No.	Sq.ft.	No.	Sq.ft.	Percent	Percent
Commercial clearcut	27.0	8.3	4.2	1.1	3.0	1.0	34.2	10.4	24.5	28.5
2M bd.ft. reserve	31.6	13.0	4.5	1.6	2.2	1.0	38.3	15.5	19.0	24.0
4M bd.ft. reserve	20.8	10.3	2.5	1.2	4.0	2.8	27.3	14.3	16.5	22.0
6M bd.ft. reserve	14.6	6.8	2.0	1.0	3.0	1.8	19.6	9.6	8.5	10.5
Check	4.0	2.6	1.5	0.6	1.2	0.7	6.6	3.9	2.0	2.5
Average	19.6	8.2	2.9	1.1	2.7	1.5	25.2	10.7		

Losses continued during the remaining 8 years, but at a greatly diminished rate. These losses were about equally divided between the last two 4-year periods.

Table 5 shows the relationship of wind losses by treatments for the 12-year study period and the 1 year (1943) in which the plots were subjected to their first severe windstorms. The heavy windfall losses of the first 4-year period were concentrated during this year of first windstorms of gale intensity. All cutover plots suffered approximately two-thirds of their total tree and basal-area mortality at this time.

Table 5.-- Wind losses by first storms, 1943, and total for the period

Treatments	Trees per acre		Basal area per acre		1943 loss as a per-cent of 12-year loss	
	12 years 1940-51	1 year 1943	12 years 1940-51	1 year 1943	No. of trees	Basal area
	No.	No.	Sq.ft.	Sq.ft.	Percent	Percent
Commercial clearcut	34.2	21.8	10.4	6.7	64.0	65.0
2M bd.ft. reserve	38.3	28.8	15.5	11.9	75.0	77.0
4M bd.ft. reserve	27.2	18.8	14.3	9.4	69.0	66.0
6M bd.ft. reserve	19.6	13.7	9.6	6.3	70.0	66.0
Check	6.6	3.4	3.9	2.3	52.0	59.0
Average	25.2	17.3	10.7	7.3	69.0	68.0

The plots had comparatively little windfall in the first 3 years (1940-42) after logging. These early losses were proportional to those ¡ incurred during the last 8 years of the study period.

In tables 4 and 5 there is the suggestion of a trend between losses and intensity of cutting, especially in the 2,000, 4,000, and 6,000 board-foot reserve treatments. Losses, in both number of trees and basal area, appear to increase with an increase in the severity of cutting, the relation being fairly constant for all periods. This apparent trend is more pronounced when losses for all periods are combined and expressed as a percent of post-treatment (1940) growing stock as shown in the last two columns of table 4. But analysis of the data showed that wind losses were not significantly related to either severity of cutting or reserve basal area.

DISCUSSION

The results of this study show that for a period of 12 growing seasons following logging, windfall in partially cut old-growth lodgepole pine was very heavy. The loss of more than 16 percent of the residual growing stock resulted in little or no positive net increment. The uncut check plots produced a greater amount of net annual increment per acre than any of the treated plots. It can therefore be concluded that partial cutting does not stimulate growth of the residual stand in mature lodgepole pine forests. Since the species reproduced adequately under all degrees of cutting used, it appears that clearcutting and complete utilization of the slow-growing overstory, so that it can be replaced by a vigorous new stand, is to be recommended.

Studies on the Fraser Experimental Forest have shown that damaging winds in the area come mainly from the west. When all severe winds blow in the same direction, one storm of gale intensity is likely to take down most of the vulnerable trees with it. The remaining stand will be largely of windfirm stems. Only a few of them are likely to be blown down by subsequent storms.

This study confirms that contention. The cutting plots were subjected twice to storms of gale intensity in 1943. The most severe storm hit in January when the ground was dry and snow covered; the second in May when the ground was wet and loose from melting snow. Windfall was heavy and concentrated at the time of these two windstorms. Following the big blowdown in 1943 the stand was made up of the more windfirm trees and losses diminished greatly thereafter, despite the occurrence of a storm of gale intensity in June of 1946.

The lack of significant relationship between heavier wind losses and heavier cutting is difficult to explain. It is logical that such a relationship should exist. The more trees removed the more the remaining stand is exposed. A partial explanation of the failure to show a significant relationship may be due to topographic variation. The topography of the study area was very broken up as figure 1 shows. Some of the plots straddle ridges; others lie partly on slopes and in valley bottoms.

SUMMARY

Wind was by far the most important of the natural agencies causing mortality, regardless of the method of cutting. Windfall was heaviest at the time of first severe windstorms and diminished thereafter, despite subsequent windstorms of great intensity. The amount of wind loss was related to the intensity of cutting only in a general way. Irregular topography apparently caused considerable variation in the amount of wind loss.

Insect losses were second in importance to wind, but accounted for only about one-fifth of the tree and basal-area losses during the 12-year period. These losses were related to the intensity of cutting in the same general way as wind losses, although the check plots suffered correspondingly heavier losses. Higher insect losses would be expected on the check plots because of the preponderance of low-vigor trees.

Losses from miscellaneous causes were minor.

MRP
11·4/12

MRP
11·3/14

A
F
C
U
I

Lum
Koto
CAT
U.S.
[19
Jan 2

Juniper c
Arnold, J
CAT310(
U.S. Dep
[18] j
Jan 22, 2

Thinning por
Gaines, Edw
CAT310057(
U.S. Departi

ATRB
1/23/14

ATRB
1/24/14

Mortality following partial cutting in virgin lodgepole pine
Alexander, Robert R;Rocky Mountain Forest and Range Experimer
CAT31005703
U S. Department of Agriculture, National Agricultural Library

[16] mortalityfollowi16alex

Jan 22, 2014

CPSIA information can be obtained
at www.ICGtesting.com
Printed in the USA
BVHW08s1101170918
527713BV00021B/602/P